THEN & NOW

MUHLENBERG COUNTY

In 1930, a slower pace and simple games formed family bonds that wove generations together in a timeless fashion. In this photograph, 14-year-old Harry Anderson, of Gus, plays a game of marbles with his grandfather, Leonard Hackett Anderson. (H. L. Anderson Jr.)

THEN & NOW

MUHLENBERG COUNTY

Cleo Roberson
Jan Anderson

To all the people who have ever been a part of Muhlenberg County then and now, this book is dedicated to you.

ISBN 978-0-7385-8570-3

Library of Congress Control Number: 2009939707

Published by Arcadia Publishing
Charleston SC, Chicago IL, Portsmouth NH, San Francisco CA

Printed in the United States of America

For all general information contact Arcadia Publishing at:
Telephone 843-853-2070
Fax 843-853-0044
E-mail sales@arcadiapublishing.com
For customer service and orders:
Toll-Free 1-888-313-2665

Visit us on the Internet at www.arcadiapublishing.com

On the Front Cover: The first Muhlenberg County Courthouse, built in 1800, was a log structure in Greenville, Kentucky. It was replaced by a brick structure in 1812, followed by a larger brick building on the same site in 1835. In 1907, a new courthouse was built on Main Street for approximately $88,000. The 102-year-old-courthouse once again underwent revitalization in 2009. The $6.3-million renovation of the facility is due for completion in 2010. (Then, Muhlenberg Libraries; Now, Steve Martin.)

On the Back Cover: Sitting on their father's grave in 1922, the Kirtley boys survived the early loss of their father, John M. Kirtley Sr., to become exemplary citizens. John Sr. was diagnosed with appendicitis while on a market trip to St. Louis. Upon returning home, he was sent to Owensboro, where, following surgery, he succumbed to gangrene. He left behind his 25-year-old wife, Susie (Campbell) Kirtley, and four sons—from left to right, Shirley, John Jr., William (Iney), and Bernard (Red) Kirtley. (Marilyn Kirtley.)

Contents

Acknowledgments

We wish to thank everyone who generously shared a story, a picture, a treasured memento, or an encouraging word with us as we worked on this project. A book like this is never the product of any one or two people. It is a combined effort among all those who wish to see treasured fragments of our collective history captured and catalogued so they can be shared with others. Special thanks go to the Greenville Harbin Memorial Library and Genealogy Annex staff members Annise Williams, Teresa Graham, and Connie Wallace; the Muhlenberg County Central City Library and staff; the Duncan Center and Shara Snodgrass; the *Times-Argus* and staff members Mark Stone, Richard Deavers, Amy Stewart, Debby Harris; the *Leader News* staff and Jowanna Bandy; Christine Hinsey; Mollie Alward; Patsy and Bobby Dunn; Barry Duvall; Teresa Duvall; Lee Michael Jenkins; Thomas Brizendine; Larry Sparks; Martha Roberts; Marilyn Kirtley; the Martin estate; Peggy Williams; Brenda Wade; Keith and Genon Putnam; Danny and Brenda Walker; Elizabeth and Darrel Gentry; Ron Poole; JoNell Stewart; Ted Curtis; Terrill Vincent; Julie Hansen; H. L. Anderson Jr.; Don Roberson; Karen Walters; Jack Simpson; Hallie and Bill Whitmer; Mike Richardson; Donna Richardson; Edna McSpedden; Sandra Cather; Bry Roberson; Curt Roberson; Lin Cisney; Paul Moore; Peggy Stovall; Larry and Ann Elliott; the Hargis Harvey family; the Brian Schindler family; the Chad Guffy family; Kathy Vinson; Howard Hawkins; Casey Hambrick; Bremen Elementary School staff; Venita Ray; Carol McClure; Gail Warren; JoAnne Stovall; Judge/Executive Rick Newman; Rockford's staff; Laura Montgomery; Linda Moore; David Wortham; Wes Johnson; fire chief Jerry Aders; deputy chief John Laster; Lila Lassiter; and Betty Wells.

Introduction

Tucked away in the heart of Western Kentucky is a county unique in its history and future. Its lush forests, abundant wildlife, and free-flowing rivers and streams beckoned to the victors of the Revolutionary War who claimed thousands of acres in land grants for service to their country. With them came wives, children, slaves, a strong work ethic, and a sense of duty to family and country. Soldiers who had served under Gen. Peter Muhlenberg in the Revolutionary War so admired their fearless leader that they agreed to name the newly formed county in his honor when it was officially established in 1798.

Where seasoned soldiers settled, others soon followed, feeling safe living in proximity to those who knew how to protect themselves and others. County history tells of an early land where panthers, wolves, wild turkeys, and deer were commonplace. Native Americans were few in the area, having left long before most settlers arrived. Though the region was rich in resources, families were forced by isolation to be independent and self-reliant. Family farms were the backbone of the newly settled land, and church services were often private family gatherings. But as settlements grew into towns, churches were built and served as a venue for both spiritual and social interactions.

In 1820, William McLean discovered coal on his family's farm. He was the first to realize that local coal could be a major fuel produced in the county. Drift banks were established to help provide blacksmiths with the fuel they called "rock coal" to differentiate it from the charcoal they had previously used in their forges. Along with coal, iron was also discovered in the county. But attempts to mine and use it came to an unsuccessful end at the Airdrie settlement, where Sir Robert Alexander of Scotland invested $300,000 in 1855 to build and run an iron furnace. His impatience with his miners and their old-world methods caused him to abandon his investment, but the Scottish employees stayed behind to start new lives and occupations in the county. Alyette Buckner and Cadwalder Churchill began another smelting furnace in 1838 that was also abandoned after shipping costs for the ore became prohibitive to realizing a profit from the labor.

Coal became more lucrative for the county as time passed. Over 231,000 tons was produced for sale by 1890. By 1900, production had doubled, and by 1911, the county was producing over 2.5 million tons of coal a year. The effects of the Industrial Revolution had finally changed the face of Muhlenberg County. Railroads crosshatched the land, and mines and miners would become famous in song across the nation in 1946, when Merle Travis wrote about the dangers of the mines in the lyrics to "Sixteen Tons" and "Dark as a Dungeon."

Coal mining, always a dangerous profession, has had some positive outcomes for the county in ways that could not have been foreseen in the beginning. The abundance of coal brought industry to the area in the form of the Kentucky Utilities Plant and the Tennessee Valley Authority's Paradise fossil fuel plant. The TVA plant consumes 20,000 tons of coal daily, which in turn has created more jobs for the county. In 1972, a coal severance tax was imposed; in 2009, the tax amounted to $1,145,953 for the county. This tax revenue varies yearly and is used for structural development as well as to improve roads, schools, medical facilities, and other necessities of growth and maintenance—like the new Muhlenberg County Emergency Complex currently being built on the bypass that will house all emergency personnel, ambulances, and the 911 system and operators, as well as provide a conference room for emergency management meetings and ham radio operations.

Major employers in the county have long been the board of education, Muhlenberg Community Hospital, and the Tennessee Valley Authority, but new industry has continued to arrive in the form of Dyno Nobel, Ensign-Bickford Aerospace and Defense, the Kentucky National Guard Wendell H. Ford Regional Training Center, and in 2008, Gourmet Express. In 2009, the local airport celebrated its completed renovation and expansion with a 4,000-square-foot terminal addition and an expanded 2,500 feet of taxiway along with the ability to house 20 to 23 planes in an enlarged hangar. The old terminal now houses PHI Air Medical, an on-site emergency helicopter flight service available for inter-facility transport of critically injured or ill patients 24 hours a day, seven days a week. Muhlenberg County Community College opened in Central City in 2001, making two-year associate and technical degrees available in the county for the first time.

Though the county may look rural, it is unique in its ability to offer special areas of interest that appeal to everyone. Lake Malone State Park in Dunmor offers camping, fishing, and boating; the county's Rails to Trails has 6 miles of paved rail walkway for biking or walking between Greenville and Central City; the Duncan Cultural Center offers a museum of the coal history of the county and monthly programs and exhibits along with memorabilia of Muhlenberg County native and movie star Warren Oates; the Palace Theatre offers entertainment with regularly scheduled productions, and the Merle Travis Museum and Music Center in Powderly is the scene of musical productions by well-known performers from all over the country. Paradise Park in Powderly contains a historic shotgun house, the Merle Travis birthplace, the Paradise Park Museum, and the original Springridge School House. The Four Legends fountain in Drakesboro honors native thumb pickers Kennedy Jones, Mose Rager, Merle Travis, and Ike Everly; and the House of Onyx on Greenville's Main Street encompasses almost a city block where people come from all over the world to buy and trade gemstones. Last but not least, the newest addition to the county has been a new convention center in Central City, complete with an indoor pool, gym, racquetball courts, and a full selection of exercise equipment to meet everyone's fitness needs.

Though the county has been best known for its record-setting coal production and for being the home of the Everly Brothers, it has also been home to generous citizens like Iris Givens, Felix Martin Jr., Hamilton Duncan, Clyde (Wee) Brown, Tom Shaver, Jim Walker, Pat Morgan, Sam Jarvis, and Tom Brizendine, just to name a few, who have given freely of their time, money, and resources to enhance the lives of those who live here. Not a large county, with only about 32,000 residents, there is a unity of spirit here where tornadoes and isolating ice storms bring neighbors together to care for one another and share whatever they have. A visit to our county is a reminder of how good small-town living can be in the right place—when its essence is extraordinary! Some things just get better with time. Welcome to Muhlenberg County as we have prepared it for you—Then and Now.

CHAPTER 1

Community and Kindred Spirits

Felix E. Martin Jr., seen here around 1930, grew up to be a generous philanthropist to his home county, Muhlenberg. Upon his death on November 15, 2007, Felix left $50 million for the county's economic and cultural development and the establishment of educational, youth, substance abuse, and health and human service programs. (Martin estate.)

Felix E. Martin Jr. (right), who ranked 29th in 2008 among American's top donors, stipulated that the bulk of his estate should benefit the county where his family had lived since 1805. His grandfather, Rufus Martin, established a tobacco export business in Greenville and a dry goods company, later run by Felix's father. Community members and county officials stand in front of the Duncan Cultural Center marquee (above) commemorating Martin's philanthropy to the county in 2008. (Then, Martin estate; Now, *Times-Argus*.)

Main Street in Greenville, Kentucky, basks in the glow of renovation (below) following the completion of the "Paint the Town" project in 2009. Storefronts on the first block of town were restored to their former 1940s and 1950s commercial facades with the help of volunteers, merchants, and grant monies. Above, an ox team and mules stand harnessed to wagons on Greenville's muddy Main Street in front of the Cohen Brothers' store in 1900. (Then, Muhlenberg Libraries; Now, Jan Anderson.)

On an Easter Sunday in Muhlenberg County in 1954 above, families leave the Greenville Methodist Church dressed in their Sunday best. New churches grow to meet community needs, and hard hats take the place of Easter bonnets in 2009 as community representatives and members of the First Missionary Baptist Church wield shovels at the ground-breaking ceremonies on Oak Street. Gathered for the ceremony are, from left to right, Terence Minor, pastor; Peggy Williams, Old National Bank president; Allison Bradford; Ernestine Robinson; and Dorothy Dillard. (Then, Julie Hansen; Now, *Times-Argus*.)

Above, the 2009–2010 Lady Mustangs basketball team, coached by Mike Harper (absent), represents the countywide consolidation of seven schools under one roof in the Muhlenberg County High School system. Team members are, from left to right, (first row) Whitney Gunn, Aliah Fueller, Hannah Renolds, Megan Sallee, Sara Gabbard, Amber Griffith, and Hope Marigny; (second row) Kaitlyn Walley, Amiea Summers, Brittany Brothers, Macy Groves, Cara Daughtery, and Christina McDonald. Below, the Central City varsity basketball team poses with coach Delmas Gish (right) in 1947. (Then, Ted Curtis; Now, Mark Stone.)

Below, Central City's southwest Broad Street traffic in 1900 consists of horses with riders and a few loose cows wandering leisurely down the main thoroughfare. Children and older pedestrians have stopped to enjoy the unusual scene. The same view has greatly changed in 2010 (above), as depicted by the grandeur of The Courtyard, an assisted living facility that opened in 1999 with 38 apartments and cost over $3 million to complete. (Then, Muhlenberg Libraries; Now, Jan Anderson.)

This peaceful tree-lined sidewalk scene (left) near 151 North Main Street in Greenville exemplifies small-town life in 1905 as an unidentified lady strolls with her parasol toward town. An aerial shot of the same Greenville street in 2009 (below) reflects the town's growth, with a new judicial building in place next to the domeless courthouse undergoing renovation. The post office and newly constructed jail are located behind the courthouse. (Then, Muhlenberg Libraries; Now, Danny Walker.)

Everyone loves the fair and a chance to dunk a teacher. Above, Popular Central City coach and principal George Taylor bravely sits on the Dunk-A-Roo during the county fair in 1960 to raise money for the school. The year 2000 brings the county fair to town right on schedule. And children still love a good time and a good ride, as evidenced by the two unidentified girls below enjoying the merry-go-round and the sights and sounds that surround them. (Then, JoNell Stewart; Now, *Times-Argus*.)

CHAPTER 2

Transportation and Transformation

In 1927, the Red Goose bus made two round trips daily to Owensboro by way of Bremen, Sacramento, and Calhoun. Roy Smith owned the bus, and Aaron Dukes was the driver. A one-way trip took more than two hours. Roy also operated a taxi service out of the Old Inn Hotel, which later became the Greenville Hotel. (Muhlenberg Libraries.)

Below, gasoline rationing during World War II required Square Deal Grocery owner Pack Stovall (left) and Bob Hudspeth (third from left) to park their truck and use a horse and wagon once again for grocery deliveries in Greenville. In 2009, the same store on Main Street in Greenville (above) has a brightly restored original Diet Rite Cola sign above it. The new gift store On Main is located in the original Square Deal Building, built in 1944. (Then, Peggy Clark; Now, Jan Anderson.)

At left, Freddie Crick Jr. uses a credit card to pay for gasoline prior to refueling his own vehicle at a Huck's self-serve pump in 2009. Hargis Harvey (above), owner and operator of the Gulf service station in Greenville in 1970, waits for a customer. At that time, full service at a gasoline station was expected to accompany a fill-up, including an oil check, windshield washing, and tire pressure check—all delivered with a smile. (Then, Harvey family; Now, Jan Anderson.)

The 1942 picture at right shows four-year-old Joe Ben Tucker lining his toy car up with his father's fleet of ambulances and hearses at the Tucker Funeral Home in Central City. Below, four-year-old Keenan Durall demonstrates similar intentions as he pushes his Jeep 4x4 across the yard to put it in place along with his other vehicles in 2007. (Then, Joe Ben Tucker; Now, Terrill Vincent.)

Above, Brady Dragoo gets set for an airplane ride courtesy of pilot Danny Walker during Young Eagles week at the Muhlenberg County Airport in 2007. The Young Eagles Program, sponsored by local pilots, gives children ages 7 to 17 a "hands-on" flight experience accompanied by their parents. Shown at the Greenville Air Port below posing by the plane he was learning to fly around 1944, Felix E. Martin Jr. is another young pilot in the making. (Then, Duncan Center; Now, Danny Walker.)

Below, two unidentified young ladies are waiting patiently in a horse and buggy with whip at hand around 1885. The stone steps on the right were used to assist in mounting and dismounting horses. A different style of travel for young ladies is shown above in 2007, as, from left to right, Lauren, Bailey, and Sarah Walker prepare to embark on a trip over the fields and through the woods on their gasoline-powered four-wheeler. (Then, Muhlenberg Libraries; Now, Danny and Brenda Walker.)

In Muhlenberg County in 2009 (below), the tradition of family and friends that makes America great lives on. From left to right, Michael Schindler, Isaiah Guffy, Dawson Guffy, and Caroline Schindler play on a John Deere four-wheeler. While the dress styles differ in the 1925 group of friends at play above, the smiles all say, "Life is good!" They are, from left to right, Jane Lloyd Hunter, Edward Yonts, Oliver Yonts, Ann Taylor Mulligan, and Jean Taylor Thomson. (Then, Julie Hansen; Now, Jan Anderson.)

Above, Emma (left) and Ethelwyn Duncan (center), holding baby Andrew, wait patiently as they prepare for an outing in their early 1900s convertible. Andrew Duncan Sr. (right) cranks the car to get it started for their journey. The Roberson grandparents load their 2005 PT Cruiser convertible (below) for a short family trip. No hand cranking is required for this vehicle. Family members preparing for the trip are, from left to right, Fancy, Cleo, Katie, Nick, Jake, Colby, and Don Roberson. (Then, Duncan Center; Now, Jan Anderson.)

In 2008 (left), cruising continues to be the thing to do every Labor Day weekend, when classic cars get together in Central City for the Everly Brothers Rock 'n' Roll Cruise-In. This event began in 2002 and continues to grow every year, hosting approximately 350 cars and their owners in 2008. Below, Larry Sparks (left) and friend Alton McIntosh (right) take Sparks's 16th birthday present, a Pontiac Chieftain convertible, for a cruise in 1951. (Then, Larry Sparks; Now, *Times-Argus*.)

Members of the Buck Childress family are shown below on the banks of the Green River near the Airdrie settlement in 1916. The family lived in the small town of Paradise, where the Tennessee Valley Paradise Fossil Plant was begun in 1959. With the steam plant in the background above, Joseph Anderson (left), Paden Hadley (center), and H. L. Anderson Jr. watch barges hauling coal to the TVA from the exact location where the Childress family gathered 94 years earlier. (Then, Nat Noffsinger; Now, Aaron Anderson.)

CHAPTER 3

Technology and Business

The Greenville Corner Restaurant, located on Main Street at West Main Cross Street, was operated as a full restaurant by five different owners and as a soda fountain by seven other owners. Also known as Hale's Corner, Cotton's Corner, Camera Corner, and Jones Café, it was a favorite gathering place for teens through the early 1980s. The building was demolished in 1985. (Larry Sparks.)

The J. S. Ward family of Central City poses above with baby Jack Simpson around 1944, when phones in the area were still party lines. By 1996, Jack (below), a 1959 graduate of Central City High School, was becoming involved in the communications field, serving as president of satellite communications for Scientific Atlanta. He traveled around the world helping to establish satellite television and phone service in areas where no cable or wire connections existed because of the topography. (Both, Jack Simpson.)

At left, Hallie Whitmer gives her husband, Bill, a tender kiss on his forehead on their 59th wedding anniversary in 2009 at their home. Along with Joe and Donna Whitmer, Bill and Hallie owned Broadway Jewelry in Central City for 60 years, from March 1948 to December 2008. Bill and his brother Joe opened the popular jewelry and gift store with $3,500 in savings from their paper routes. Bill participates in a training session below. (Then, Hallie Whitmer; Now, Jan Anderson.)

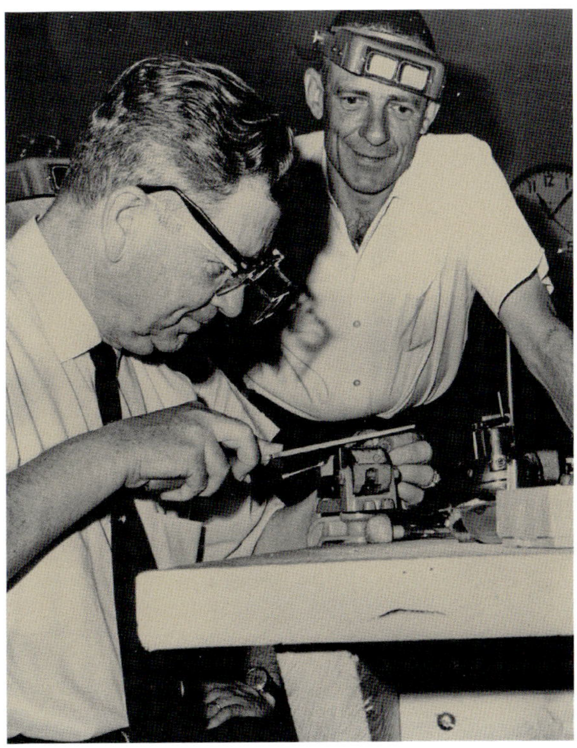

Shelby and Leona Stewart and son Shelby Gene Stewart started the first of their three grocery stores, below, in 1944 at the Y in Central City. In 1954, Stewart's Groceries became Independent Grocers Alliance (IGA) stores. The Stewarts owned these IGA locations until 2001. Small-town stores and delis still feed the community, as evidenced by Charles "Preacher" Nelson, right, purchasing a lunchtime sandwich "to go" at Nicholas' Market and Grocery in Bremen. (Then, Nell Jane Stewart; Now, Jan Anderson.)

In 2010 (below), Classic Lady women's clothing store stands in the vicinity of Gamble's previous location. Posing in and in front of the business are, from left to right, Joy Dozer, Leah Dunn, Betty Webb, Judy Soderling, and Sheila Bivins. At left, Billy Rose (left) and Joe Grable (right) stand in front of Gamble's Firestone Store on Greenville's Main Street around 1955. Grable continued the family business tradition started by his father, Moody Grable, who owned and operated Drakesboro's theater, grocery, and Chili Bowl until his death in 1936. (Then, Muhlenberg Libraries; Now, Jan Anderson.)

Above, unidentified telephone operators stay busy at the switchboard as they direct incoming calls for telephone customers in 1926. A large fan cools the room for them on a hot summer day. Technology introduced by the phone systems continues to expand, evidenced by second graders at Bremen Elementary School (right) busy at their computer stations mastering the intricacies of keyboarding and communications applications. In the classroom are, from left to right, Michaela Campbell, Clay Embry, Allie Butterworth, and instructional monitor Beth Ellis. (Then, Muhlenberg Libraries; Now, Jan Anderson.)

At left, Howard Hawkins, associate manger of Greenville's IGA grocery, assists Casey Hambrick and her children as Hambrick chooses a frozen meal from the Gourmet Express display. Gourmet Express became operational in the county in 2008 as a wholesaler and retailer of high quality, complete frozen dinners. Frozen dinners were rare in Leonard Sparks's Greenville Grocery in 1947 (below), but canned and dry goods as well as fresh vegetables were abundant. Posing behind the counter, Thelma Cash Sparks proudly holds daughter Judy Sparks. (Then, Larry Sparks; Now, Jan Anderson.)

Around 1940, the Arbuckel Café in Greenville (below) was one of the favorite eating spots for locals as well as travelers boarding trains at the depot. From left to right above in 2010, Bill Alward, Sheila Brownlee (owner), and Molly Alward enjoy dinner conversation at the Purple Onion Restaurant and Sports Bar in Central City. The Purple Onion was opened in 1995 by Ron and Sheila Brownlee, who also own and operate Cinema IV next door. (Then, Muhlenberg Libraries; Now, Jan Anderson.)

CHAPTER 4

ART AND ENTERTAINMENT

The art of advertising and entertainment was not lost on the owners of the W. G. Duncan Coal Company, as they placed their ads, featuring "figures talk," to boost business. Shopping ladies in bustles and hats had stopping power as they perused the department store selections at a dream location around 1900. (Christine Hinsey.)

Everyone loves a parade, as demonstrated by the huge 1940s crowd above lining the sidewalks to watch the floats, cars, and bands as they make their way down Broad Street in Central City. Parade activities continue to fill the streets of the county in 2007, below, as Cordie Johnson, grand marshal of the Greenville Christmas Parade, talks with city administrator Ben VanHooser prior to the start of the annual festivities. (Then JoNell Stewart; Now, Paul Moore.)

The South Elementary dulcimer group above performed for Greenville Elementary students and the Fun Over Forty Club in 2008. The group, which clogged and played the dulcimers and spoons for audiences, includes, from left to right, (first row) Kristin Dickerson, Autumn Deason, Carter Johnson, and Callie Newman; (second row) Tyler O'Bannon, Brooke Benton, McKenzie Johnson, Haven Diehl, and Abby Coin. Unidentified members of the Central City High School Band, below, dress warmly for an outside concert around 1929. (Then, Muhlenberg Libraries; Now, *Times-Argus.*)

Below, John Brizendine (left), Francis Cisney (center), and Wayne Cisney portray historical characters during Greenville's Sesquicentennial Celebration in 1948. Sixty years later in 2008 (right), Leslie England (left) and Jeff Dickinson take the stage as a coal miner's wife and her husband. In the early 1900s, the Greenville Mercantile Company on Main Street was converted to the Palace Theatre, where local performances and plays continue to be produced. (Then, Shara Snodgrass; Now, Christine Hinsey.)

Home of the Legends thumbpicking weekend brings star attractions to the Merle Travis Music Center. Celebrating below with 1,500 other attendees and performers are, from left to right, (first row) Sheila Bivins, Joyce Stevens, Marilyn Kirtley, and Steve Rector; (second row) Terry Bivins, Al Hudson, and Joe Hudson. Shown above with his family in 1923, seven-year-old Merle Travis (left) became famous for his singing and songwriting, but his unique guitar thumbpicking style was his most emulated gift. The Travis Center honors his contribution to music. (Then, Muhlenberg Libraries; Now, *Times-Argus*.)

Members of the Rhythm Masters, pictured above in 1962, are, from left to right, Anthony Batsel, Philip Stone Jr., Jackie Simpson, and Darrel Young. They were popular performers at the youth center dances in Central City. In 2008, Greenville's Zeke Walters (right) took first place for the second year in a row in the Bluegrass Division of the Kentucky state banjo competition. Zeke and his band, County Line Bluegrass, pay tribute to the pioneers of bluegrass like Flatts and Scruggs and Bill Monroe. (Then, Ted Curtis; Now, *Times-Argus*.)

Above, patrons above enjoy the food, music, and company at Rockford's Place, a new restaurant and music shop that opened in Greenville in 2009. Rockford's is in the renovated building that was the local YMCA in 1909, built by the philanthropy of Max Weir. In 1921 (left), the building housed Dexter's Hardware, and later it became a clothing store with offices on the top floor. Hugh Lovell, sitting on the far right above, was an employee of Dexter's as a young man. (Then, Christine Hinsey; Now, Jan Anderson.)

Below, Bill McSpedden (kneeling in center) and cast take a bow after a full musical performance on Greenville's Palace Theatre stage around 1955. The stage at the Palace continues to welcome performers of all ages and sizes (right). Different productions are scheduled continually throughout the year for public entertainment. Rebecca Shepherd (left) plays the Cat in the Hat to Alora Snodgrass's JoJo the Who during a production featuring the well-known mischief-maker created by Dr. Seuss. (Then, Muhlenberg Libraries; Now, Shara Snodgrass.)

Below, Hamilton Duncan Sr. visits with, from left to right, Jan Anderson, Virginia Cummins, and Donna Richardson, three nationally recognized artists, during festivities at the Duncan Center in 1992. Duncan donated his unique home to the city of Greenville, and it is used today as a museum as well as a cultural, historical, and educational center by county residents. Celebrating his heritage, a young Hamilton Duncan (left) wears a kilt in the Duncan family Scottish plaid. (Then, Duncan Center; Now, Jan Anderson.)

At right, Sisters Jean (left) and Ann Taylor (right) wear their swimsuits and caps as they enjoy a day on the water in 1923. Aerodynamically designed swimsuits and caps of a modern Muhlenberg County swim team (below) differ greatly from the swim wear of the 1920s. These Muhlenberg County Rockets are a part of the USA Kentucky Swim Club and practice daily at the Central City Convention Center pool, where they have year-round access to the water. (Then, Julie Hansen; Now, Amy Anderson.)

CHAPTER 5

EDUCATION AND EDIFICATION

In the beginning of Muhlenberg County's history, schools were only open a few months each year, and no formal instruction went beyond primary work until 1850. Children walked to school and were aware that keen switches would be used as necessary to maintain discipline. These unidentified Weir School children pose happily for a picture with their classmates in 1942. (Muhlenberg Libraries.)

Below, Model Ts and other sleek cars of the day await students' dismissal from the school started as Greenville Female Academy around 1920. The building later became the property of the Greenville School District, to be used for primary and secondary education. Educational opportunities continue to expand for the county's citizens with the completion of the Muhlenberg Community College campus in Central City in 2001 (above), which enabled students to receive associate and vocational degrees locally. (Then, Muhlenberg Libraries; Now, Jan Anderson.)

The South Carrolton home nestling peacefully on the banks of the Green River below was built by Mike and Kathy Gilles in 1988. They bought the property from Raymond Bolin and Richard Campbell and proceeded to tear down the crumbling remains of the Bittersweet Tavern in front of their home site. In 1938 (above), the tavern was the hub of social gatherings for the pre–World War II generation who gathered there to eat, dance, and enjoy the orchestras. (Then, Muhlenberg Libraries; Now, Jan Anderson.)

Representing grades one though eight, 50 students gather at the Drake School above for a class photograph in 1915. A log cabin measuring 20 feet by 20 feet, this school was the first located in Drakesboro and was built around 1852. Children like the Head Start class below in 2000 have the opportunity to learn outside the classroom. Here they explore the exciting unknown of a fire truck courtesy of firemen Keith and Shawn Putnam. (Then, Gail Warren; Now, Keith Putman.)

Above, seniors at Muhlenberg County High School in 2010 work on science projects with up-to-date equipment as instructor Peggy Stewart helps prepare them for advanced college courses. A 1985 Greenville High School chemistry class below enjoys a demonstration by teacher Walter Silvey. They are, from left to right, (first row) Mike Boggess, Mike Diaz, Scott Griffin, Lori Kindrick, and Lori Loughran; (second row) Ross Jones, Sean Ginsburg, Susan Ebling, Lori Lile, teacher Walter Silvey, Curt Roberson, and unidentified; (third row) unidentified, Jamie Pogue, and Rick Thompson. (Then, *Times-Argus;* Now, Jan Anderson.)

As bundled spectators line the sidewalks awaiting Santa Claus, a horse and wagon pull Christmas parade participants down Broad Street on a cold winter day in Central City in 1956 below. Riding in the wagon are Sharon Williams (left) and Mary K. Morman (center). Heavily clothed people line the same Broad Street above in 2009 for a chance to see Santa Claus as he waves to the crowd. Leading the way for Santa are David Higgs (left) and David Richey. (Then, Muhlenberg Libraries; Now, *Times-Argus*.)

Above, in 1952, friends await a ride to Conservation Camp. Identified in no particular order are Danny Harkins, Sonny Harkins, Brenda Newman, Anne Kirkpatrick, Ann Bippus, Julie Dwyer, Kay Shutt, Ann Hood, Janie Chumley, JoAnna Fox, Janie McDonald, and Billie Sue Brasher. Below, in 2001, Tom Lewis (right), a retired conservation officer, and Jerry Bailey scout out an area surrounding Lake Malone to prepare an adventure for members of the Conservation Club. (Then, Muhlenberg Libraries; Now, *Leader News.*)

Alexander Cather (right) and sister Marion pose with their bicycles around 1929 in their front yard in Central City. Alexander grew up to be a dedicated teacher and mentor to hundreds of students who graduated from Central City High School, where he taught from 1946 to 1981. He is shown below receiving a plaque on his retirement in 1998 commending him for years of service as chairman of the board at Drakesboro United Methodist Church. (Now, Sandra Cather; then, Sandra Cather.)

Above, Central City Golden Tide All-American Corky Withrow (far right), who also played for the St. Louis Cardinals baseball team, poses with other well-known 1950s-era basketball legends in 2008. They are, from left to right, King Kelly Coleman, Howie Crittenden, and Fred Maggard. Muhlenberg County all-district basketball players pose together below in 1963. They are, from left to right, (first row) Eddie Devine, Ronnie Maddox, unidentified, Melvin VanHooser, Gary McDonald, and Rodney Kirtley; (second row) two unidentified, Joe Pentecost, John Elliott, Tommy Stovall, and unidentified. (Then, Marilyn Kirtley; Now, *Times-Argus*.)

The Greenville High School football team of 1984 (below) represents a segment of the "First in Fifty." The county had been without a football team from 1930 until this new squad was formed 50 years later. Consolidation of the Muhlenberg County high schools led to the formation of the Mustangs football team. The 2009 team (above) reflects the greater number of athletes available to participate in sports. (Then, Muhlenberg Libraries; Now, *Times-Argus*.)

A tradition of service continues in 2008 as Capt. Steve Boswell (left), of the Muhlenberg North High School ROTC color guard, and ROTC major Jordan Rice perform for Central City Elementary students. A 1950 group of Central City patrol boys stands ready for action above. They are, from left to right, (first row) Boyce Reeves, unidentified, Larry Mercer, and unidentified; (second row) Charles Napier, Bill Greenwood, unidentified, and Larry Devine; (third row) Ronnie McDowell, two unidentified, and Jerry LaMastus; (fourth row) principal Clay Sharp and newspaperman Larry Stone. (Then, Ted Curtis; Now, *Times-Argus*.)

Michele Bowling (above), curriculum specialist at Central City Elementary School, poses as the Cat in the Hat to hold the attention of students as she reads to them during the Head Start fun night at the school in 2007. Innovative teachers have always used creativity to stimulate students' minds. Revered teacher and mentor to many, Irma Long (right) stands in front of the Greenville High School building in this 1940s image. (Then, Muhlenberg Libraries; Now, *Times-Argus*.)

Above, around 1930, four unidentified Hughes Kirk High School girls in gym suits hold badminton and basketball equipment. Styles and form have changed by 2008, with aggressive play and trendy uniforms and equipment. Markie Smith (left) of the Muhlenberg Rage slides in safe at third while the opposing catcher (center) grabs for the ball. Umpire Jimmy Casebier (right) makes the call. (Then, Muhlenberg Libraries; Now, Mark Stone.)

The Central City High School built in 1925 (below) is barely recognizable, as the $2.8-million wellness center and convention center (above) replaces all of the older structure except for the original gym and band room, which were incorporated into the newer building. Taking advantage of exercise equipment in the new center in 2009 are, from left to right, Ann Griffin, Sue Burch, Buddy Burch, unidentified, and Dallas Miller. The new wellness center includes a pool, racquetball courts, and the latest exercise equipment. (Then, David Wortham; Now, Jan Anderson.)

Below, members of the Central City High School graduating class of 1959 are shown in 2009 at a friend's home prior to celebrating their 50th reunion at the Purple Onion Restaurant in Central City. The photograph includes 18 of the original class members. As teenagers, students of the class of 1959 are dressed in gowns and suits (above) for a formal dance sponsored by the school and local organizations. (Then, Ted Curtis; Now, Paul Moore.)

In 2009 (below), plays like the Christmas story continue to be a learning experience for children as well as a source of enjoyment for their families. Performances at church or school always heightened the fun of participation for children, as evidenced during the 1948 play above at Greenville Grade School. Performers include, from left to right, Kenny Dukes, Peggy Simpson, Steven Shaw, Dottie Carver, Judy Wilcox, Aloma Adler, Jimmy Cox, Roger Nofsinger, Julie Thomson, Tommy Dockins, and Jimmy Anderson (with the cart). (Then, Anderson family; Now, Jan Anderson.)

Below, Prof. James K. Patterson, husband of Lucy Wing, became president of the Presbyterial Academy of Greenville in 1856. The academy grew rapidly until the Civil War, when many students joined the army and the school closed. From 1869 to 1910, Patterson served as the first president of the State University in Lexington, which later became the University of Kentucky. Dr. Judith Rhodes of Central City (left) has been president of the Madisonville Community College system since 1998. (Then, Muhlenberg Libraries; Now, *Times-Argus.*)

"All things old are new again" is proven true as the $6.3-million courthouse renovations continue with a crane lifting the dome into place on top of the remodeled structure on March 9, 2010. The sidewalk clock shows the time to be 11:32 a.m. The 1907 courthouse construction (below) was underway with scaffolding surrounding the structure and men on top without safety harnesses. The 1907 project was completed at a cost of approximately $88,000. (Then, Christine Hinsey; Now, Jan Anderson.)

6

CHAPTER

MILITARY AND COMMUNITY SERVICE

In 1944 in Bexleyheath, England, Edna Woodley married Army Air Corpsman Bill McSpedden. One of 70,000 British war brides, Edna immigrated to the United States after the war. She arrived on the *Queen Mary* with firstborn daughter Donna in her arms. She and Bill moved to Muhlenberg County, where they raised three daughters—Donna, Helen, and Bea. (Donna Richardson.)

In 1943, with suitcase in hand, Ted Curtis Sr. prepares for deployment during World War II. He is accompanied by his wife, Nellie, and son, Ted Jr., as they stroll down a street in Riverside, California, toward an awaiting ship. In 2009, below, the 1957 Central City High School graduate Ted Curtis Jr. is immersed in history and photography as he works to collect valuable memorabilia and historical artifacts to share with others. (Then, Ted Curtis; Now, Jan Anderson.)

Above, Korean Conflict veterans gather at the Muhlenberg County courthouse to reminisce on Veterans Day, November 5, 2005. They are, from left to right, (first row) unidentified, Norman Ashby, unidentified, Norman Carr, unidentified, Vernon Brothers, and Clifford Deering; (second row) four unidentified, Felix Martin Jr., David Simpson, and Bob Ed Vick. Below, Harold "Truck" Evitts (left) and an unidentified friend are dressed for the bitter cold of combat in Korea around 1952. (Then, Larry Sparks; Now, Muhlenberg Libraries.)

Below, Felix E. Martin Sr., center, and unidentified members of his section operate the wireless radio used for communications during World War I. Transportation and operation of the portable set, used to give advanced warning and relay commands to fellow soldiers, required 10 mounted men and 4 pack mules. Above, National Guardsmen use the latest communication technologies while participating in a field tactical operations center receiving and disseminating information during a training exercise in 2008. (Then, Martin Estate; Now, Spc. Michael Pfaff.)

At left, a family of volunteer firefighters serves daily along with other dedicated professionals and volunteers to preserve the lives and property of Muhlenberg County residents. From left to right are Keith, Shawn, and Genon Putnam. Equipment and tactics have changed drastically since the introduction of the steam-powered fire engine above around 1856. Present-day trucks, along with fire-retardant Nomex suits and helmets that withstand 1,500-degree temperatures, now help protect firefighters from the heat and flames. (Then, Christine Hinsey; Now, Genon Putnam.)

Three members of the Jenkins family (above) have carried the mail on the same route in Central City. Lee Michael Jenkins (right) currently has the route; his father, Jimmy Lee Jenkins (center), delivered the mail in Central City until his retirement; and his grandfather, James Lee Jenkins (left), died from a heart attack on his route in 1946 at age 42. After 32 years of employment at the Greenville post office, Bobby Dunn (right) clocks out on his last day of work in 1992. (Then, Lee Jenkins; Now, Patsy Dunn.)

Above, unidentified police officers on duty during Sky Fest 2009 at the Muhlenberg County Airport talk with Willard Keith (left) and former mayor Ruthie Lewis (center). Officers of the county's police and sheriff's departments are on duty 24-7 to perform routine duties and meet emergency needs as they arise. Below, a nostalgic scene depicts Greenville police officer Chester Putnam in 1960 performing the routine and now obsolete duty of collecting change from a parking meter on Main Street. (Then, Muhlenberg Libraries; Now, Jan Anderson.)

Below, the Muhlenberg County Bookmobile visits a Martwick family in 1960 as Peggy Williams stands in the doorway. This service provided rural families with access to books and educational materials. Providing needed library services continues in the county, now without a bookmobile but through the Golden Hearts outreach program, through which books are delivered by library staff members to homebound and institutionalized patrons as well as to schools. Above, Tina Cobb (left), a library outreach member, delivers books to Sarah Wester at Wester's home. (Then, Peggy Williams; Now, Wes Johnson.)

Joe Richardson and brother Lewis "Shines" were soldiers during World War II. Having received no word about his brother for two years, Joe heard a USO broadcast naming participants in a baseball game to be played at nearby Nuremberg Stadium. He hurriedly drove to the field to find Shines behind home plate, and a joyful reunion followed. Joe greets fans in 1948 below. At left, the Richardson brothers in 1928 are, from left to right, (first row) Joe, Robert, and George; (second row) Lewis "Shines" and William. (Mike Richardson.)

Max Weir (right), one of the first benefactors to the growing town of Greenville, left $7,500 to the YMCA upon his death in 1904. In 2008, retired businessman Tom Brizendine donated $100,000 toward development of a 12-acre park in Greenville named for Brizendine. He is pictured below with friends and other benefactors to the park. They are, from left to right, Ben VanHooser, Roderick Thompson Sr., Shelby Gene Stewert, Tom Brizendine, Stone Eaves, and Greenville mayor Ed DeArmond. (Then, Muhlenberg Libraries; Now, *Times-Argus.*)

CHAPTER 7

HARDSHIPS AND KINSHIPS

This slave cabin was constructed about 1840 on the Dr. R. C. Frazier farm in Powderly. Tradition states that Col. William Campbell, the founder of Greenville, brought the first slaves into Muhlenberg County. Slaves were usually housed on their owners' properties. The 1860 census reports 9,101 whites, 40 free colored, and 1,584 slaves living in the county. (Christine Hinsey.)

Sisters Margaret (left) and Mary Taylor (right), and their brother Tom Taylor (center), an engineer, joined the service during World War I. Margaret and Tom were separated from Mary, who served at military hospitals in New Jersey, England, and France. When Mary returned, she helped establish a model health department in the county. Above, registered nurses Sue Simpson (left) and Martha Roberts (right) visit with photographer George Austin and furry entertainer as they celebrate Bicentennial Health Day at Morgan Park in 1998. (Then, Julie Hansen; Now, Muhlenberg Community Hospital.)

Below, benefactors Tom (left) and Skip Shaver (right) donated $750,000 to Muhlenberg County Community College in honor of Tom's parents, P. A. Shaver Jr. and Pauline Shaver, in 2007. An earlier benefactor to the college was county resident Lt. Comdr. Iris Givens (left), a registered nurse who served her country overseas during World War II. Upon her death at 89 in 2004, this highest-ranking county veteran bequeathed $1.48 million to the community college, the largest single gift received to date. (Then, Duncan Center; Now, *Times-Argus*.)

In 1910, the worst coal-mining explosion in the county's history at Browder claimed the lives of 35 men, not counting Dr. William Richardson (right), who received a head injury from a roof bolt as he rode out of the mine with a patient. He died 10 days later. Doctors continue to risk their lives during community disasters today, as evidenced below by the service of Graham's volunteer firefighter and chief, Dr. Brian Chaney. (Then, Mike Richardson; Now, Jan Anderson.)

Larry Elliott, the great-great-grandson of slave Adam Elliott, is pictured at left in 1991 with his wife, Ann, and children, Chad and Heather. Adam Elliott, below, fathered 72 children before receiving his freedom. In February 1866, he and Ella Wing had their relationship recognized by the court, which legitimized their union and their children. Elliott died in 1925 at around 107 years of age. Prior to their emancipation, slaves had no civil rights and could not legally marry. (Both, Elliott family.)

A familiar landmark in Midland, the Smokey Bear tree house at right has stood since the late 1940s. The tree dwelling, complete with Smokey's picture, was built as a reminder to use caution when burning fields in forested areas. Smokey Bear's campaign began as a World War II program to alert citizens to enemy attempts at setting fires in coastal areas. Above, Eli Shemwell, age four, wears a fireman's helmet as he tours a fire truck promoting fire awareness and safety. (Then, Danny Walker; Now, *Times-Argus.*)

World War II veterans gather below in 2005 at the county courthouse. They are, in no particular order, Kenneth Robison, Leroy Hendrix, Tom Brizendine, Charles Shipp, William Vincent, Bill Whitmer, Guy Overby, Lee Moore, Owen Grace, Elmo Oates, Robert Tucker, Paul Bethel, Harold Streets, Bill Winter, Dilford Holmes, Bob Ed Vick, Charles DeArmond, Roy Darity, John Eaves, Adrian Lee, Obbae Jones, James Steel, and Ernest McElwain. Above, in 1909, county Civil War veterans gather for a reunion with photographer Orien Roark in front. (Then, Carol McClure; Now, Paul Moore.)

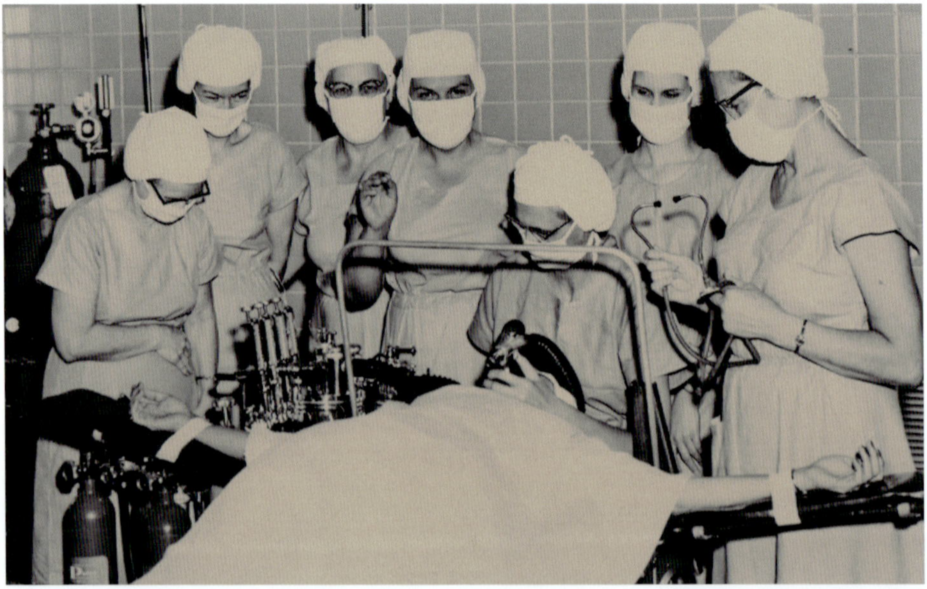

Above, surgical nurses surround a "patient" posed for a demonstration of the latest equipment in the new surgical suite at Muhlenberg Community Hospital in 1961. They are, from left to right, Pauline Milam, Thelma Putnam, Pearl Strong, R.N., Bessie Vincent, Estelle Ross, R.N., Glenda Vincent, and Lola Mundy. The 2010 photograph below shows the latest equipment on hand in Dr. Mary Brown's office as she (left) and her assistant Mary Lee Doss (right) perform a procedure with computer screens in the background. (Then, Ted Curtis; Now, Jan Anderson.)

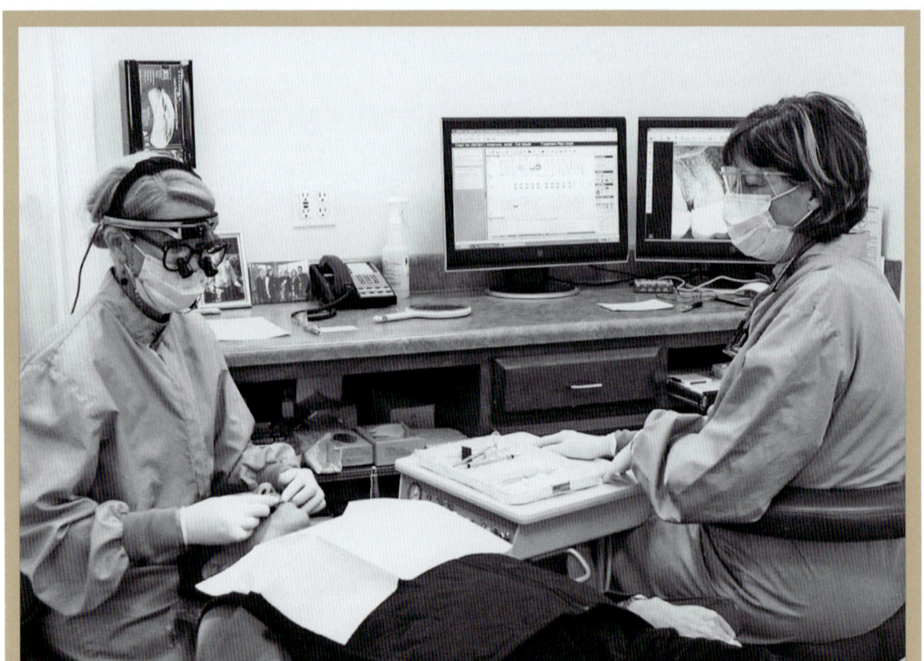

Above, wife and husband pharmacists Elizabeth and Darrel Gentry enjoy Muhlenberg County Airport Sky Fest 2009 activities. The Gentrys opened their first pharmacy in 1972 and now own four drugstores in the county, at Central City, Greenville, Powderly, and Beechmont.

Pharmacist Joe Durham, below, works behind the counter of Durham Drugs in Central City in 1958. As a pharmacist in the 1950s, Durham saw the development of synthetic pharmaceuticals begin, which changed the face of medicine. (Then, JoNell Stewart; Now, Jan Anderson.)

At right, little Taylor cousins Jean (right) and Jane share a moment of concerned affection on a summer day in Muhlenberg County in 1922. Above, children of the Care Club continue to cooperate in the spirit of compassion and concern as they raise money for the Relay for Life campaign in 2008. The club's total monetary contribution for the year from bake sales and door-to-door collections was $300. Members include, from left to right, Grace and Haleigh Haustein, Keely Culbertson, Stephanie Oglesby, and Allie Culbertson. (Then, Julie Hansen; Now, *Times-Argus*.)

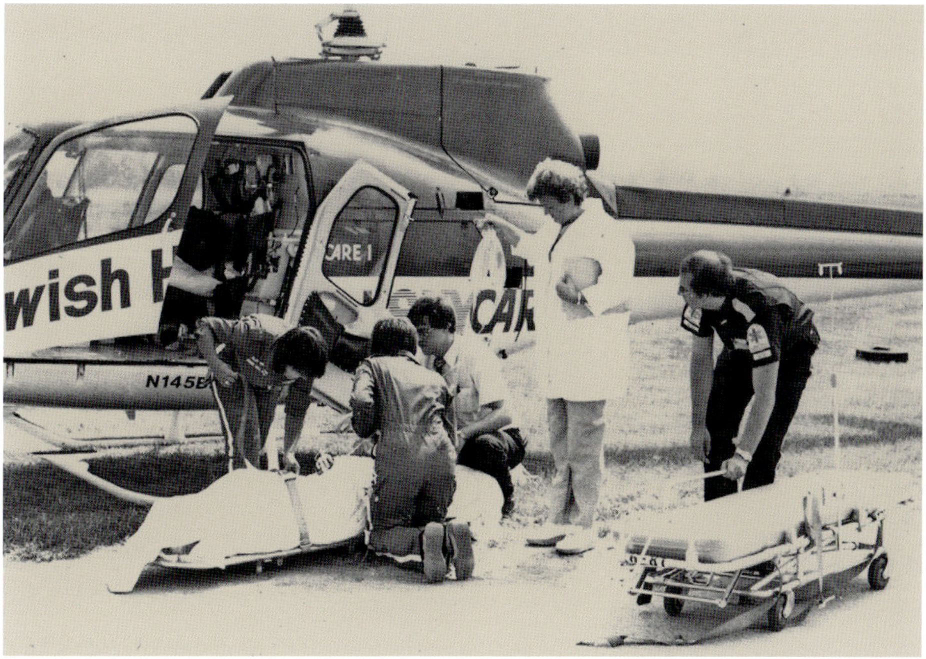

Below, PHI Air Medical opened its newest base at the Muhlenberg County Airport in June 2008. The new helicopter service provides 24-hour inter-facility emergency transfers as well as pre-hospital scene response in the county. Employees of the new service are, from left to right, Billy Dukes, Chandra Herman, Donna DeArmond, Barry Groves, Nicole Ginsburg, and Josh Brand. Above, Glenda Newman, R.N., and paramedic Danny Yonts transfer a patient from Muhlenberg Community Hospital to an awaiting Louisville Jewish Hospital helicopter around 1988. (Then, Muhlenberg Community Hospital; Now, *Times-Argus*.)

At right, Ras Bivins of Central City stands in the backyard of his home with two "killer" icicles that broke from his roof during the ice glaze of 1951. The glaze effect was considered the worst ice storm in the area until the winter storm of February 2009, which left the county's residents without power during freezing temperatures for two weeks. Below are pine trees with broken limbs and ice-laden power lines in the Rolling Hills subdivision in 2009. (Both, Jan Anderson.)

At left, a tornadic smoke cloud adds drama to the 2007 Geibel's pallet mill fire in Greenville. The blaze took its toll on firemen and volunteers as they worked in 100-degree temperatures battling the flames. The fire smoldered for days in the depths of the sawdust piles and required persistence on the part of the firemen to keep it under control. Watched by concerned citizens below, firefighters battle a blaze on Broad Street in Central City about 1945. (Then, Ted Curtis; Now, Meagan Chaney.)

Below, in 1959, Larry Sparks's Packard 400 sits damaged in a collapsed garage, while debris covers the truck parked outside. Tornadoes struck the county again in 2008, killing three family members at the Nolen Trailer Park, above, near Greenville. Traveling from Greenville to Central City, the F3 tornado was 325 yards wide with 160 mile-per-hour winds and affected 113 homes. Paramedic Troy Walker (left) and Don Garret (right) offer food to an unidentified victim at the Nolen Trailer Park. (Then, Larry Sparks; Now, *Times-Argus*.)

CHAPTER 8

Family and Friends

The wedding of Ethelwyn Richardson and Andrew Duncan took place in 1905. Unidentified members of the wedding party are shown posing in front of the newlyweds, who are barely visible standing on the back row. Formal gowns and tuxedos were the dress of the day for an event of this societal magnitude. (Duncan Center.)

Playing good guys and bad guys in the front yard above, three little boys—from left to right, Oscar Wheeler, Charles Taylor, and Eddie Countzler—emulate the popular western cowboys of the day in 1939. Cowboys remain popular heroes still today, as evidenced by Central City First Baptist Church's 2007 Valentine's Day banquet theme—cowboys, cowgirls, and cupid. Below, a cardboard cutout of Roy Rogers smiles at Richard Shaver, in costume beside him. (Then, Julie Hansen; Now, *Times-Argus.*)

For children, make believe and "dress up" remain timeless entertainment. Above, a fairy-tale castle becomes a magical place for friends in costume in 2004 as they play at being well-dressed princesses for the day. The princesses are, from left to right, Hannah Clark, Hope Clark, Keely Dennis, Eden Hadley, and Lela Grace Anderson. Below, flower girls and a ring bearer are dressed up for real as they pose angelically prior to Mary and Roy Wells's wedding in 1924. The children are, from left to right, Jean Taylor, Ann Taylor, Jane Taylor, and George Albert Kelly. (Then, Julie Hansen; Now, Jan Anderson.)

Below, Fannie Clark finds a restful moment in a makeshift playhouse around 1900 as she holds her doll beside her and poses for the postcard photograph that was sent to her grandfather in Morton's Gap. Her faithful dog lies at her feet to protect her in the rustic hideaway. Today's little girls, above, enjoy time together in a beautiful custom playhouse complete with a porch and flowerbeds. They are, from left to right, Jessie, Sarah, and Audrey Anderson. (Then, Gail Warren; Now, Jan Anderson.)

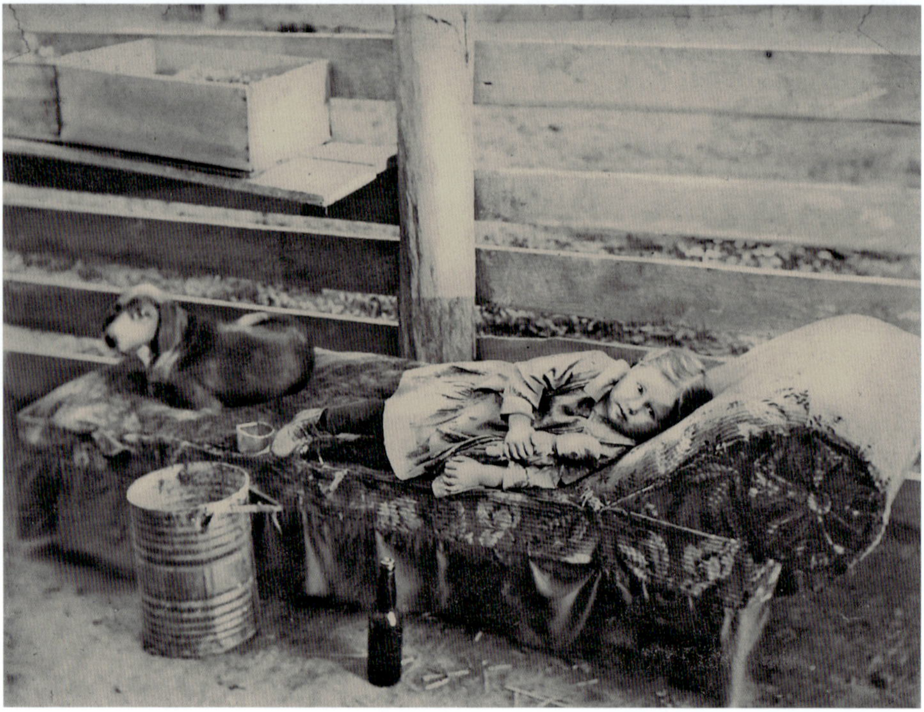

Famous for their catfish and sawdust pie, Jean and Nat Noffsinger have been serving customers at their restaurant and marina on Lake Malone, below, since 1982. With seating for 150, the Shady Cliff Restaurant, Lodge, and Marina is popular with customers from Muhlenberg, Todd, and Logan Counties. Above, Joe Lovell (right) waits for the day's specials at the Davis brothers' Trolley Café on South Main Street in Greenville in 1928. The Davis brothers are standing behind the counter. (Then, Muhlenberg Libraries; Now, *Times-Argus*.)

A family reunion always means enough good food to satisfy everyone's appetite. Above, around 1910, the Corley families have gathered on their farm with the standard Southern fare of fried chicken, green beans, mashed potatoes, corn, pies, and washtubs full of iced drinks. A picnic in Muhlenberg County still brings families and friends together over good food. At right, in 2007, Hilda Schultz (left), Owen Schultz (center), and Len Bard are enjoying the conversation and casual cuisine. (Then, Joanne Stovall; Now, *Times-Argus.*)

At left, a family from Rochester gathers at McDonald's, a popular choice in Greenville for an evening meal. Job requirements and children's busy school and extracurricular schedules force families to eat on the run in 2009. The tranquil scene below in 1945 shows an extended family of grandparents, children, and grandchildren gathered around the dining table in their home and enjoying a leisurely sit-down meal. The table is beautifully decorated for the occasion. (Then, Muhlenberg Libraries; Now, Jan Anderson.)